NOME POEMS

Nome Poems

Ken Waldman

WEST END PRESS

Acknowledgments

Some of these poems have appeared in the following magazines and journals:

Aethlon, Artful Dodge, Beloit Poetry Journal, Blue Mesa Review, Chiron Review, Convolvulus, Flyway Literary Review, High Plains Literary Review, International Poetry Review, Many Mountains Moving, Owen Wister Review, Pearl, Pemmican, Poet Lore, Pudding, Rag Mag, Redneck Review, Sidewalks, South Dakota Review, Swamp Root, Talking River Review.

First edition, April 2000
ISBN: 0-931122-98-8

Book and cover design by Nancy Woodard
Front cover photo by Kate Salisbury

Distributed by University of New Mexico Press

West End Press • P.O. Box 27334 • Albuquerque, New Mexico 87125

Contents

Letter Sent to Mark Rozema

The snow's over. Holding an envelope
I walk the thirty yards uphill
to my mailbox. Everything is heavy,
white, except the trees and sky—
they're different kinds of silver.

I raise the flag, place the letter
in the box—this letter
addressed to a friend who used to walk
miles in snow, and in walking
decided to enter the priesthood.

I walk down my driveway. *My life
keeps changing*, I wrote, *but now
I know where I have to go—
and I'm uneasy. Who'd have thought
bush Alaska had such pull.*

Passing my cabin door, I decide
to walk further and explore
how this first winter snow
has blanketed the trail
descending into the gorge.

I

Welcome to Nome

Where thirty-five hundred stumblers
reckon the edge;

where feckless ones jump;

where the garbage barge drops
salt, cold, driftwood, rust;

where six-year-olds spit;

where holy ghosts drink
tequila and schnapps;

where sad jokes sleep;

where open sores catch
cheap flights home;

where the soul smarts;

where wind flings storms, dust
clings, sky slings paint;

where Siberia speaks;

where what was and what is
disappear;

where God blinks;

where tundra, ice, horizon
rise into space.

Shorty's Fiddle

My first Nome Sunday, Harry North, Sr.
waggled a finger, reeled me in
off Front Street, another tomcod
snagged on his invisible line.
"Not a one in town since Shorty,"
North mumbled in a hiss, which fit
what I'd heard: The man worked
like a snake, loved to make people
squirm, meant to be cryptic and cruel,
was evil. I'd talked to him Friday,
needed a room—he owned most of town—
and when he offered "a goddamn steal
you can't refuse," I told him
I'd think about it. "Too bad, fiddler,"
he'd spluttered. "The rent just rose."

Now I stood in his little shop
that joined his bar where Eskimos
and whites found their truth in drink
and puke, where the dancers swayed
and jerked to stale smoke and disco hits.
"Just love fiddle music—you can jam
with my boys," North muttered,
blinked lidded eyes, tugged
my sleeve. "Come on, boy. *Come on.*
Shorty's fiddle's hanging in the cellar.
Twelve years since it's been played—
since Shorty left for Nashville.
Promised he'd come home for it
some day. Told me to hold it.
Come see for yourself, boy."

I followed North downstairs through one,
two, three hallways lined with beer
and booze, to a shadowy storeroom
with toilet and sink. Taking fiddle
and bow off the wall, he grunted,
and thrust the instrument toward me.

3

I held that fiddle, coaxed all
but the G into tune, grabbed Shorty's bow,
tightened it, then ripped a medley
of slippery bluesy old modal ones
from the Ozarks, faster and faster
until I made that murderous devil
rapist dance, made him shake,
made him groan as I slid up the strings,
Harry North, Sr., wicked puppet.

Anecdotes

I

She was fifteen, no mother
or father to speak of.
No husband either.
So when she flew to Nome
to deliver what would be
an eight-pound boy,
when she saw me, her old
seventh grade teacher,
she waved and asked me
to be with her in labor.

I watched from behind
the doctor. After the birth,
new son nestled on her belly,
the doctor momentarily gone,
she turned to me, smiled
weakly. *I need chew.*
Be a good girl and go
to the store. Copenhagen,
Red Man—either will do.

II

On Front Street, a tourist—
white-haired and hearty,
he looked like someone
from the East Coast—
motioned, then asked whether
I was from here. Shrugging,
I nodded. *A lucky young woman,*
he said. He'd always wanted
to visit Nome. Now he was retired,
a former high school principal
And you, he asked. *What do you do?*

I teach, I said. The ex-principal
froze. *The Eskimos*, he whispered
as one walked by. *The Eskimos.*
Tell me about the Eskimos.
Tell me if they're savage.

That whisper—
the wind had taken an axe
and split us.

III

See this? The saloon keeper
pointed to finely ground rock
spread on paper. Lifting the sheet,
gently folding, he let the bits
settle, then rolled paper and flakes
like a foot-long cigarette.
Gold, the saloon keeper said.
This is what men die for.
This is Nome. Now go on.
He funneled the contents to a jar.
If you're not drinking,
I don't want you around.

Gold, the new schoolteacher thought
as she slipped out the barroom,
let the door slam. She had heard
the saloon keeper owned
half of Nome, had gotten rich
on Native drinking, had once killed
a man, kicking him to death
with his boots.

The next day the saloon keeper
motioned the new schoolteacher inside,
set a tequila in front of her.
You want the secret of success?
Live in a place you like.
Do work you enjoy.

IV

I asked my students
to write the saddest thing
that ever happened.
One girl wrote: *Mommy*
flew to Nome to drink.
Daddy stayed home. Friday night
Uncle Tony came over.
They had a drink.
Then they went to Uncle Jim's
to play cards. The fire
went out. In the morning
the baby was dead.

Nome Post Office

Here where a cold July rain
pours for months, where January
lasts a decade, where one warm
sunny June midnight balances
all that is winter, I set my watch
by the late-afternoon mail run,
that dependable daily pulse
of Nome comings and goings
like a collective umbilical cord
to the future. Today I crossed
Front Street at 4:30, squeezing
between the double-parked trucks,
holding my breath from the fumes.
Exchanging five or six hellos,
then sidestepping the Eskimo elders
standing dazed like lost commuters,
I dug in my pocket for the chain,
fit key in lock, opened my box,
snatched a yellow slip delivered
that instant by a bear claw of a hand
that scratched. Grasping the tag
marked PACKAGE, my scraped fingers
dripped blood on paper and floor
as I took my place, and waited
at the end of a line that snaked
around a corner. An hour later
people ahead claimed the window
had closed, and would reopen Sunday
at dawn. Fine, I replied, knowing
I had forever. And forever was now.

Small Planes Near Nome

I

For fifty years,
each time a plane
flew over the village,
the woman muttered
an Eskimo curse, shook
both fists upward.
The day of her funeral
two planes crashed.

II

The Eskimo elder,
a minister, blessed
each voyage to Nome
by opening his palms,
then clasping fingers
tight like a basket.
He'd say: *Your plane
is safe in my hands.*

III

When an Eskimo is lost
alone in a blizzard,
a red plane will land.
The pilot, a smiling
white man, will gesture
to hurry. An Eskimo
who boards that plane
will never return.

Smart Girl

Turning fourteen , the oldest, you learn
to cope with a crowded and smelly
house, the beginning of one more
eight-month winter, your village
at the frozen tip of a distant island.
Smart girl. You steal a key,
sneak from fifth period study hall,
and coax your boyfriend to lie
on top of you on the broken sofa
in the upstairs storage room.

It only takes minutes, these trysts
you egg on until you've outwitted
them all. Smart girl. Preoccupied,
you make A's, but for the B in Health.
Three weeks after your mother has
her sixth, you deliver your boy
mid-July at the hospital in Nome.
You're happy through summer,
a real mom almost. So precocious.
Then back to school, a sophomore.

Winter's Five Miles Away

Division Street's gravel
is sloshed, puddles
too greedy to freeze.
A soaked October refuses
to snap, and no one wins
but the day bartender,
Harve, a wry Eskimo
who pours his boss
a third double tequila,
pockets a ten buck tip.
The manager's hammered.
Worm-brown eyes, stained
teeth, a face pocked
like the muck. *Whaddayasay,*
he mumbles, big shotglass
drained. *Whaddayasay
I drink to motherfuckin'
Nome and the goddamn wind.*

Turning, Harve empties
an ashtray, wipes the bar.
Tomorrow, the Eskimo snorts,
will kick like a moose.

Nome Trooper

Baby-faced and bald, he wandered bush Alaska
staking a claim: a banjo, a small plane, a wife
who strummed guitar and mandolin back-up.
At last settled beside a salmon creek four miles
out of Nome, his house the next-to-last
on that stretch of gravel and ice, he was happy
to have a fiddle over. We played a few tunes,
talked about bootleggers and booze, Natives
and whites, local politics, agreed and disagreed
how to solve the most recent Juneau mess,
might have jammed like that all night
until he served milk and cookies, slid a tape
into the machine. Real music now, he announced,
flicking off the lamp, lighting a candle.
I listened to that ten-minute Star-Spangled Banner
banjo solo as I'd so often listened to my father:
Slipping into sad reverie, I gazed out the window,
caught a plain round moon too simple to believe.

Nome Bypass Road

The freak November of no snow
while some laced skates to scrape
figure-eights on a pond just east
of town, twice a week I biked
the bypass, a two-mile gravel spur
linking Nome's east end to asphalt
north of the regional hospital.

Wind-chill below zero, layered
in polypropylene and wool, I pedaled
the loop clockwise, pleased
to put even a little distance
between myself and a home town
that always seemed so ridiculous
once I was out of it, always

so exhaustive while in it.
Still in shape from a summer
of daily riding, I pumped hard,
sweated easily despite the cold,
amazed not by the tundra horizon
that could have been Oregon
high desert, nor by the sun's

pokey falling through a sky
that was purpling over a sea
that was freezing, nor by the ice
sticking like burrs in my beard,
but that this was the edge
of a limitless universe
and I was cycling, thrilled.

The Board of Trade Saloon

5 P.M., shuffling west
up Front Street, studying
the brilliant orange
and gold sun's plunge
into the frozen ocean's
horizon, I see an Eskimo
stumble out the BOT's
door, double over, vomit
a trail on sidewalk ice,
this thirty feet ahead.

I stand a minute,
unsure whether to attend
the man, or to pass,
pretending the problem's
not mine. South,
the half-gone sun still
blinds, and sinks a crack.
Before me, two drunks
stagger from the BOT,
drag the first inside.

I walk past the spot,
then the ivory shop,
where the BOT's owner
waves. I nod my return—
guilty—then backtrack,
sidestepping vomit,
to catch a bright sunlit line
slip from pink winter sky,
an icy view that portends
the Nome night's violence.

II

An Evening of Local Poetry
Sponsored by the Nome Arts Council

A spread of reindeer, moose,
king crab, smoked salmon,
whale meat we dip in seal oil—

Eskimo food which we wash
with Cold Duck, Budweiser,
a bottle or two of schnapps.

Nothing special here—
we speak of snow, wind,
the nature of drift.

We eat and drink as simply.

The Eye of the Cold

First-time Nome visitors see history:
a big rich minefield of stars—the far sky
an oddly proper hat for a near-wasteland
of frozen ocean, river, and hill surrounding
a cockeyed church-and-barroom outpost,
a chronically ill Alaska village that boasts
the slim charms of an almost ghost town.

Transient residents—adventure-happy traders,
teachers, state and federal workers—
see the cracked souls, Eskimo and white,
that can't face the ice. No good place to go,
no good thing to do, these broken hopes
cash checks, play bingo, drink liquor, sit
nursing their blind and shameful dread.

Long-term Nomeites, both settled and adrift,
view the sunset's improbable purples
and pinks, the stark landscape's desolate
windswept light. Huddled safe in the depths
of home, they see beyond politics—
an impenetrable flux of culture and trash—
into winter's dark mirror of gold.

Nome Magistrate

Bloodshot eyes bulging like some odd
and reconstituted steelhead or salmon,
he sat in his state office, framed
by a frozen horizon streaked in pink,
and once more wondered how in the hell
a smart, Harvard-educated, Iowa
farmboy survivor who could tie flies
and wrestle crocs had found himself
trapped in this snow-covered dogshit
arctic port. How was it, goddamn,
that he'd crossed a line, got tangled,
so was stuck here cursed, as sad a case

as those in his files. A rape to try
tomorrow on the island, no choice
but to linger this evening in the Anchor
or Nugget, mull what a whiskey or two
might cloud or stir. Goddamn,
how he longed for the utter night
of Barrow and the north Alaska coast,
where on public radio, Monday noon,
a colleague hosted a half-hour of blues
and spun mean bottleneck guitars toward
the dawn for those few proud Inupiat
music lovers distant and pure as space.

The Sunday New York Times

—for Brad Gater

A rich Alaskan inventor friend subscribes
first-class through an ex-Montana address
that, like all the old P.O. boxes,
he's kept current. For weeks
the heavy bundle's forwarded—Whitefish,
Eugene, Boulder, Santa Fe, Moab,
Flagstaff, Taos, and to Fairbanks
and beyond—the zigzagged path
the weekly retracing of my friend's
iffy decade-long search for meaning.

Like a lost tomcat, *The Sunday Times*
appears unexpectedly, eventually,
little worse for the wear, its arrival
announced by a slip in a bush P.O. box.
Approximately six weeks ripe, the paper
is digested with sourdough hotcakes, coffee,
miles and miles of tundra and sky.
My friend writes: From where I sit,
so help me god, *The Times* is the pulp
of some king fool genius fictioneer.

The Big Village

Nome's Front Street, the Manhattan
of Norton Sound, where Eskimos
from fifteen villages fly in daily
on small planes, the ninety-dollar ride
the Bering Straits equivalent
of taking a train from the Bronx.
Last night the mayor of Savoonga,
a carver unaccustomed to booze,
stumbled out the Polaris barroom,
then weaved the sidewalk mumbling:
He'd seen God. Flagging a cab,
he vomited alcohol, pancakes, blood.

Today, hung over, he'll sleep in,
miss one flight, the next, the next,
figuring he's in Nome, what the hell,
potholed streets, broken lights,
drunken Native fellowship:
the wife and eight kids can wait.
Tonight, he'll trade a small ivory dog
for a couple of pints of beer.
Tomorrow, again sleeping past two,
he'll dream Jesus has risen,
a face blank and cold
as the moon at minus ten.

Wesley

Still in third grade,
ten-year-old Wesley,
the one who's nothing
but spaghetti. Tall
for his age, thin,
spaghetti-colored hair,
he sits in the back,
collapsed at his desk,
his t-shirts tie-dyed
yellow, green, purple.
His dad's dead. His mom
tends bar weekend nights.
Wesley can barely read
or write. His mom says
he still pees in bed.
Wesley. No teacher
gets through, only Sue,
a pretty fourth-grader
whose dad's Indian.
Recess, they rush
to the playground
corner, the swings.
Pumping, they kick
higher, soaring,
rusty chains creaking.

Sid's Journal Check

Read out loud, Sid ordered, pointing,
and pulled the chair too close,
gray eyes widening to some lost
high. After all, Miriam, he said,
you told us to write *anything*,
and you would *love* to read it. I skimmed
several pages: a young Nome Eskimo
alone in a dismal anchorage motel room
was oiling and re-oiling his gun.
Suddenly, an ink-smeared, big-print
final paragraph: the Eskimo met a friend,
the two followed a woman to a park,
shot her, carried her to the motel room
where each took a turn fucking the corpse.
When the men killed each other, the dead
woman awoke. As I finished, Sid's whisper
sputtered like a furnace unable to fire:
I could fuck you like that, Miriam.

Sid, read your story aloud, I said.
My student stiffened, eyes gone to dead
dark bugs. No longer his teacher, Miriam,
I became one more anonymous white woman
to be hated with the rest of the landscape.

Inupiat Blood

Drunk, you chose sudden lust
that sunlit July midnight
camped outside Council,
the river trip with the blond
shop teacher, your summer beau.
After, feeling oddly filled,
snuggled beside him in the tent,
you didn't want to think.

Autumn, despite your boyfriend's
wishy-washy promises of love
and support, you quit college
in Anchorage, flew to the village.
Through months of blowing snow
and cold, you knitted, sewed,
read, visited family and friends,
made light of your beloved's freeze.

A late March evening, purple sunset,
the vision: you'd ruined your dream
of cruising med school, becoming
the first Inupiat woman surgeon
to return to the Bush. Instead
you'd remain on the Sound, take
ed classes by correspondence,
singly raise a boy, Dexter—

an A student from kindergarten,
a star athlete, an obedient son—
who'd leave home forever to flunk
from Anchorage his first semester,
marry a white, and drink. And you,
high school math and science teacher
by fate, you'd teach the algebra
of x and y, the cruel probability of z.

Runaway

Pretty if you like the mix
of Eskimo and white, Dawn,
a scrawny sixteen-year-old,
scuffles up 4th Avenue,
Anchorage, the sidewalk
an iced slide. Passing
travel agency posters
of Hawaii, she glances—
and nearly slips.
Six months pregnant,
her precarious balance:
the baby's father,
a Ft. Rich private,
won't admit; her friends
drink; her big belly
doesn't warm her,
nor does her pussycat,
a yellow tabby hidden
between sweater and shirt.
Poking her head inside
the bar, Dawn ducks
into a noon darkness
spilled with beer.

Nome Industry

Along the Bering Sea coast,
these few cluttered miles
of small houses spewing oil-
fired smoke make Nome a grim
little factory town of cold,
the sullen gray skyline
a dwarfed Detroit.

The good worker—wise
to wind-chill, layers, the way
this strange place anchors
a whole world—briskly walks
the frozen streets that open
to a dark and vast computer-
driven wilderness: the office.

Into the White

The young Siberian Yupik woman from Savoonga
had everything the June she graduated high school:
the company of beloved family; the swollen nets
at fish camp; the full scholarship to Fairbanks;
the confidence her good looks would win her
a cute white schoolteacher husband with whom
she'd one day return—this last desire so deep
she told no one, but all summer knelt in prayer
before the flowers, the berries, the birds.

Second week of college, at a dorm party
with an Inupiat ballplayer from Unalakleet,
she got drunk, spent the night. The next months,
no sleep. January, back home after flunking out,
forced to babysit five young siblings, she dreamed
of entering prison, giving birth. Instead,
she followed her great-great-grandfather's soul.
February full moon she walked out of the village
far onto the sea ice. The wind with her.

December 26, Wales

Yesterday, Christmas. Today, blizzard.
You worry, angel, Uncle Seth won't like
the ivory seal because one eye's cracked,
and Aunt Irma the fancy stoneware crockpot,
the catalog order from Utah. You worry
cousin Isaac will take the next plane to Nome
for a drunk, and cousin Shirley, the flirt,
will get pregnant again. You even worry
I won't cherish my new gold-handled knife.

Angel, let's not argue. All this worry
is bad exercise—leave it for people
unsure of their ways. Let's be thankful
for our house, our food, this village life.
Let's be thankful our love grows like grass
and has power over the air. Everything
has been provided. We need nothing more.
Today, blizzard. Time for patience.
Tomorrow, less wind, a settling into light.

III

Nome Newspaperman

From across the street, I raise my camera,
catch a man smoking a cigarette, sipping
from a big mug of coffee, waving
to one passerby, nodding to another, this
from his mid-morning perch on the step
in front of the Nugget office. That backdrop,
its foundation long tilted from permafrost,
looks like an old houseboat run aground

and taking on water. So I snap
several shots of this handsome Californian
who could go anywhere, yet chooses
to bounce from one Nome job to the next,
nights in the bars, always another drink,
another story, another week, another deadline,
another pound gained, another edition
tying his name more tightly to the cockeyed.

The sweater-clad reporter sees me then,
smiles broadly, winks, raises the burning stub
of tobacco to his lips, and tosses it down
as if a finger of vodka, chasing it
with a last slug of coffee. *Ah*, he yells,
I love this place. And makes an abrupt
about-face, pulls open the door, and disappears
inside to report the latest casualty.

Third Street, Nome

A sign of my own past's big wreck,
the Honda with shattered windshield,
dented door, and smashed front fender
stands today in drifted snow
beside an abandoned '55 Ford truck
boasting fang-like grillework. Dead
of advanced hypothermia, both rigs,
so typical of downtown Nome
trash, cheer me. Last month, soaked
by rain as I fought forty-mile wind,
I cut through that favorite lot, glanced
south two blocks where the Bering's
surf crashed into seawall rock,
and understood why I liked this town
that's beyond almost all Alaska:
The very air's wild and rushing—
every breath's a snort.

Tomorrow when I walk east
down the middle of Third, I'll peer
through the morning darkness. The Honda
and Ford will sit, murky shapes
lit by streetlight. Next corner,
waiting for the bus, a schoolgirl
will stand. I'll open my gloved palm
to wave hello. Her answer:
a big-city prostitute's hard nod.
Shuffling past, head down, my boots
sliding on ice, I'll steal a final
glimpse—and she'll glare, spit,
then raise a cigarette butt
to her shadowy lips.

The Littlest House in All of Teller

Though invited in, I begged off,
somehow troubled by a feeling
the crippled husky pup chained
to a post by the corner
of your tiny yellow dwelling
lived the healthiest life
on the lot. I did peek
inside, noticed the waterbed
covered half the floor space,
a claustrophobic arrangement
for you, your boyfriend, your son,
an eight-year-old momma's boy
gone mute from hearing you sleep
with a half-dozen abusive men
over the years. Mid-October,
windy, plastic windows flapping
like broken wings, thick clouds
threatening winter's first storm,
you, my Brevig student, and I,
your Nome college writing teacher,
until now static voices
on telephone, pen-pals who swapped
stories, stood by your front door,
and looked in each other's eyes
for a moment. Though I knew
you were unemployed, fired
from the only two jobs in town
that suited, hoped to move
to Nome, open a hair salon,
and own a three-bedroom house,
I saw you, Inupiat woman,
so lost from your nature
you took classes, drank, smoked,
wept, dreamt, slept, woke,
your daily cycle a forlorn

indiscriminate blur. And you,
if you'd have truly seen me,
your professor, I believe
you'd have found a white man
equally out of place, a nomad
unaware how his heart craved love,
how his soul demanded beauty,
how his vision sought a home.

Midnight

The time one day bleeds
into the next, I unsnap
the case, put that fiddle
under my chin, curl fingers
around the bow, and play
spooked, archaic tunes. "Hey,
you're scarin' the cats—
quit scarin' the cats,"
my housemate would shout,
the godawful scratchy squeaks
getting to him, ten years
back, the fall I started.
Ten years—thirty-five hundred

midnights, time enough
to learn two secrets: a wrist
that twitches in shuffling
pulls; a soul that flies
blind into the fingering's
notey, sliding drones.
Today I charm felines, refuse
housemates, and live a hermit
in an evil little town
where only the devil cares
I make late-night music
that taps a vein, drains
juice, transfuses.

Nine Pieces of Paper

Down to nine pieces of paper, Ken,
a failing village student wrote
late November, then stuck
that message in an envelope,
postage paid by addressee.

Eight days later (a bad storm
had grounded planes), the words
reached me a hundred miles away.
I pictured her, Lois, as I had
six weeks earlier, my visit:

a young, stout, well-meaning woman,
loud, talky, slow, bespectacled,
a mom with twin five-year-old boys,
a four-year-old girl, a husband
away. Where, she didn't know.

A recovering alcoholic, Lois
had escaped that trap
to land in another: Addicted
to bingo, she couldn't keep money,
wouldn't do mental work, lied.

Rereading her note, I wanted
to repeat what I'd told the class
time after time: Call me at home,
at the college, or use the fax.
I wanted to shake that stolid body

with the obvious: Look, Lois,
borrow paper. Or take a dollar
of your bingo money and splurge.
Or at least fill the nine pieces
you do have—yes, both sides.

On a scrap, I scrawled a quick
Keep going, Lois—you can do it,
stuffed it in a mailer with a ream
of blank sheets. And scribbled beneath
the label *Lois, this is your chance.*

Polar Bar, Nome

As my student, Nick, rose
from a shadowy far-side table,
jerkily wobbled toward the door,
we caught eyes, and I recalled
his first graded paper—fine writing
about a knife, a stabbing, a wound,
then a rapid disintegration
of story that produced an effect
I'd called "unintended experimental."
Semester-long his work had drifted
that way despite the conferences,
this part Yupik, part Inupiat student
who'd witnessed an in-family murder
before graduating eighth grade,
later entered the service, the past
three weeks missed every class.
Did I say our eyes caught? They locked
like lost twins for a crazy twisty moment,
made me think of my sad father
and his vanished drunken brother,
their quarter-century of silence,
my own fearsome shameful secrets,
before I returned to my drink.
I might have heard Nick depart mumbling
something about "ripped" and "home
to bed." Though I'd have laid odds
he was off to the Board of Trade
and would haunt that bar until close.

Village Fiddle

I toted my junker, side seam already cracked,
an old cheap box of wood that would take
the steep banks of small planes aiming
for runways, the bumps and jostles of sleds
hooked to snowmachines, the ice, the wind,
nights in the villages. Higher education
missionary, I made rounds to students' homes
(where I visited, but never fit), to liaisons'
offices (where the state-issued equipment
sometimes worked), to the local high schools
and elementaries (where I volunteered service)—
fiddle closer to my heart than the backpack
full of books. Indeed, closer to my heart
than the frozen broken truth: a bloody pump
buried in utter darkness. Quick to unsnap
the case, I scratched tunes where no one had,
played real-life old-time music to Eskimos
and the odd whites in that weathered land.
The Pied Fiddler, I might have been, gently
placing the beat-up instrument in others' hands,
giving up the bow. Good for smiles and laughs.
Random questions and comments. A third-grader:
It must be like having a dog always making noise—
you must never get lonely. A high-schooler:
Is it hard to learn? One of my college students:
Why are you out here? Where is your family?

The Victim

Once admitted, I gave up my wallet
and penknife, slung my daypack
over a shoulder, casually strolled
upstairs to bed as if registered
in a hostel. Two weeks before,
not an inkling of turmoil,
my academic life spinning out
good familiar days of teaching
and writing, sanity unquestioned
unless I were to own the despair
of the students I taught
or the dark poetry I wrote,
related shadows that plumbed
the bush Alaska winter, a gloom
no one from elsewhere can fathom.

My hospital room, institutional
in a brutal sense—the plain
linoleum floor like a grade-school
hallway, the terrible gray walls
like a small windowless office,
the two narrow beds like those
in a freshman dorm. I was greeted
by a spinsterish nurse, who frowned
and huffily wished me good-night
when I refused pills. Sorry
she hadn't stayed to talk, I changed
to a gown, eased in bed, glad
for the peace needed to open
the book I'd begun on the plane,
One Flew Over the Cuckoo's Nest,

the choice an irony I couldn't bother
mulling, for now thankful the worst
of the Seattle holiday week vacation
seemingly had eased. Christmas Eve
I'd flown in from Nome, been introduced
to a friend of a friend, a woman

for whom I felt nothing, but danced
step-by step into the most delicious
erotic rapture—and woke to find
my heart and soul ruptured, my bearing
spirited away, my juice stolen.
I slipped out hoping the anxiety
would pass with food, with friends,
with music, with sleep. Instead,
a numbed grief, between madness

and shock, settled. For hours
I rattled how I'd been mugged, raped,
slashed, shot, then filled pages—
a whole yellow legal tablet full—
with the smeary big-print scrawl, the same
scary childlike phrases over and over:
I'm Hurt and I don't know what to do,
I'm Hurt and I don't know what to do,
Help Me   Help Me   Help Me   Help Me.
My hosts, worried my nightly pacing,
my groaning, my clear and profound
suffering might break me, sat with me
as we revealed innermost shames—
old traumas, love failures, demons—
as if prattling about happy gossip.

The fifth day of mania, the emotional dump
steady as the cold misty shroud fogging
the city, my friends phoned a counselor
who made time that night, saw me briefly,
then suggested immediate hospitalization,
my jumpy wild logic so driverless
he ended the session a half-hour early
to call for an empty bed. That quickly
I was en route, my voluntary compliance
hinging on the fancy I was to enter
a spa-like facility where I'd enjoy
non-stop mothering, my private suite
a well-lit, modern, natural sanctuary
staffed by wise, compassionate healers
who'd nurse me through crisis.

I didn't feel crazy, thumbing pages,
stifling a yawn, setting down the book,
my slow breezy drift to sleep
only a little odd, like that fall's
Labor Day snow. Everything is fine,
I whispered, positive by seeking rescue,
despite my absolute miscalculation,
I'd skirted further collapse. Next,
having dreamed a wooden beam crashed
through the ceiling, smashing my computer
and skull to dust, I woke moaning
how I couldn't breathe, mustn't write,
wouldn't last the coming hour
because something too big to understand,
some giant maniac, was after me.

I ran the corridor toward an aide,
a short neat man sitting at a desk
riffling a magazine. I can't sleep
and need to talk, I panted, hearing
a ghost inside murmur I shouldn't
confide—this man couldn't help.
Leading me down the hall to a lounge,
thin fingers on my shoulder, he asked
what was wrong. You're gay, I announced,
so stunned I'd broken the taboo
my teeth clattered. No, he replied.
Yes yes, I maintained, my voice
from somewhere deeper than the stray
frantic conscious. No, he repeated
testily, long whiplike tongue snapping,

and even if I were, I wouldn't tell—
now, what is it you want to talk about?
But I'd already torn loose, my bare
slender feet squeaking the hall
as if my bones, my skin, or the floor
needed oiling. Hopping back to bed,
I remembered Ozzy, a decent guy
no one in my graduate school class
befriended, a top journalist recently

found dead off Kodiak, a boating mishap.
Ozzy was gay. Mourning Ozzy, a man
who liked me, whose help I refused
out of fear, I found myself relaxing,
breathing for the first time in a week,
wholly taking in what I didn't know

I had denied: affection for Ozzy.
Falling asleep, picturing Ozzy's land
off Farmers Loop in Fairbanks, birches
silvered with snow, then Abigail's
snug log cabin on top of Ester Dome,
November nights cuddling under quilts,
the perfect embodiment of heat,
while outside the lights, the clarity,
the outhouse, the cold, her husky,
Sookie, yelping at a backfiring truck,
I bolted awake, the image of a wolf
shackled at the ankle, the sense
my own right foot lay paralyzed,
a cut through a nerve. For minutes
I couldn't move the foot, or the leg,

but once I wiggled my toes, willed
ankle joints to flex, I recognized
if I didn't rise out of bed at once
I might not leave this mental ward
for a long time. Peering out
the door, when I spotted the nurse
who had met my arrival now plodding
up the hall like a fat and wheezy
Virgin Mary, the double chin,
plump cheeks, gray eyes heavier
than rain clouds made me wave her
in my room, ask that she sit
beside me on the bed and to then
hold my hand. I knew she would,
and once she took my fingers, I gushed

to this confessor my life story:
how my mother abused me, how my father
beat me, how no mentor ever saw me,
how bad luck dogged me, how my love—
Abigail—betrayed me, how my work
in Nome was killing me, how a dumb
one-night stand shook me, how
my deadened groin deranged me, how
I feared I'd never have sex again,
how I raced from the aide
because I thought he was gay,
how I dreamed my ankle was shackled
but now I could walk fine
so could I please have my wallet
and penknife because I was leaving.

Look honey, the nurse said gently,
face opening to a gap-toothed smile.
I don't know where your deep pain
fits in God's plan, but this wing's
a fine place, Dr. Gates can help you,
and if you don't mind my saying
I don't know why you're so worked up
over sex—I'm fifty-five, free
of filthy diseases, and beholden
to the Almighty for every good thing.
Stay here and you'll learn lessons
from the good book. If you're as smart
as you say, I'm sure one fine day
you'll leave here, Lord willing,
to serve mankind. Now, I have a pill. . . .

Crazy or not, I told her I'd let
no nurses, not even a good soul
pious as herself, administer pills,
let no doctor with a name like Gates
into my head, let no more time pass
in this building—I had to leave,

I was through being a victim.
She said only I'd have to wait
until seven—the wallet and penknife
were locked downstairs until next shift—
then lifted herself and waddled out.
I quickly changed clothes, stashed
the novel in my pack, returned
to the lounge, where I stood
by a window, gazed east

into darkness, and pictured myself
at dawn pocketing my belongings,
pushing open door after door
until I was striding north
up University Way, whistling,
stopping for orange juice and eggs,
next sauntering west, happy, alive,
a full recovery, a triumphant
return flight home to rural Alaska
where I'd honor my contract,
then move on. That voice within
cautioned I still had to buck
one last icy season before I'd ride
clearing sky, spring-like weather,
and mount the brilliant far heights.

IV

Resolution

The first January day I wake
to fine dry snow blowing
like needles, visibility
near zero, I'll unchain you,
Molly, half-wolf ex-lead dog pet,
you, my gift from an Eskimo, Vic,
who'd told me few white men were wild
enough to survive rural Alaska—
and give me a sled dog too headstrong to pull.

Molly, you'll shake, jump, your blue eyes
up-close like flashlit gems, your teeth
primeval carvings. You'll run, feet sinking
in powder, mine sinking in chase.
How to tell you:
This winter's made me a beast, Molly,
a lonely man as trapped between cultures
as you are between breeds,
an angry man unfit for love
or for life outside this village.

To change, Molly, I must follow you
to the end of one more twenty-hour night,
to a patch of windblown river ice.
When I call, Molly, you must turn.
With my left hand collaring you,
my right hand on the trigger, my gun
pressed to your skull, I'll shoot.
Quickly I'll gut you, Molly,
and plow my hands in squishy heat.
I'll bury you in a drift, Molly.
Your blood will come with me.

January Flight: Nome to Kotzebue

On that half-hour hop
I might have been covering
the width of Dakota—
a vast snow-heavy tundra
like common badlands—

but for the sun, that
crazy bush Alaska sun
rising with a yawn
at 10 A.M., then
imperceptibly falling

lazily back in bed,
its light flattening
to a fiery line
on the horizon
before rising once more,

the bounce into sky,
a blinding ball
sparkling divinely
as my shadow flapped
and shot into day.

Irma

Wolf to me is warm ruff over parka,
she wrote, her rough village poetry
an unintended strip of gristle
in three pages of litter. Irma.
Slitted eyes, heavy moon face,
a half-second off. I glimpsed her
once in a Nome grocery store entry,
tough Shaktoolik girl hanging out
drunk, like many. Next day, class,
she called in from prison, shared
her work, wholly incomprehensible
but for a sentence about her uncle—
Mouth of rotten teeth, his talk
a good fearing man spryly present.
Irma. I heard said in her village
God shorts all people—that's how
we learn love. Why we need family.

Dreaming of Crab

One night in Nome
we steamed king crabs,
feasted on meat
sweet as lobster
as we lightly dipped
legs in herb butter
after cracking shells.

Later, making love
on the living room rug
beside the piano,
we were distracted
by the dancing clatter
of leftover crab claws
that, like starfish,

had somehow regenerated
to full-sized whole
and now scuttled
like mutant cockroaches,
knocking table legs,
chair legs, walls, before
resettling on plates.

If it was your dream,
you'd fear the cancer
that plagued your mother
for years. My dream,
I see the resurrection
of the king crabs
as a call to gather

crabs and pot at once,
ride on snowmachine
to our fishing place,
and drop the crabs home.
There, beneath sea ice
the crustaceans will sink,
at peace among their own.

Babysitting, St. Lawrence Island

In Gambell, where the Natives speak
Siberian Yupik, "babysitting"—
the *b* and *s* sounds slippery
as seal oil—is all I translate
of the usual guttural crush of tongue.

Spoken mostly by women under seventeen,
the word means, roughly, "We live here,
because we were born here and there is
nowhere else we can go, so we sit
with love, and look after our own."

The Visitation

I'd been expecting her, the old Eskimo
who stumbled inside my Nome living room
at 3 A.M. that March night, and groaned:
The dogs, help me get away from the dogs.

She wandered the house until she stood
frozen at the foot of my bed, her face
just past full, like the moon that lit it.
She moaned: The dogs, save me from the dogs.

I've called a cab, I told her. The dogs—
please you've got to help me, she groaned.
There *are* no dogs, I told her. The dogs,
she moaned a last time, disappearing

in shadows. Next minute, a quick beep
of horn. A yelp. I rushed to the door.
Outside, footprints in fresh snow, wind,
a gray form whelping three wolves.

Nome Calendar

Minus twenty, little wind, my dawdle
the perfect pace, tonight I walked
the last half-mile home from work,
content I'd finally discovered
Nome's beguiling gift. Two years
living alone in this unsophisticated
end-of-the-world tundra compound,
too busy analyzing my mission
as young college writing instructor
out to save a dying culture,
I'd scuffed over the gritty
dry ice and packed crunchy snow
unaware there was even a present
to miss. Instead, I'd poked fun
at this ingrown and eccentric
northwest Alaska coast community
that lacked bookstore, eye doctor,
and flower shop that last spring
proclaimed itself the gateway
to Eastern Siberia; instead,
I'd coolly observed the notorious
Front Street dead-end bar scene:
a New Year's Eve without January,
a Mardi Gras without Lent; instead,
I'd stood apart and pointed,
thinking myself above the place
because no one else seemed to see,
and as teacher I honored truth.
A pity I took so long to perceive
why, with so much flat empty space
just out of town, Nome's grid
was crammed, a surreal arctic slum
of rustic two-story cabins sandwiched
between shacks that slept nine.

Tonight, strolling past house
after house, the boilers blasting,
as I watched a slow breath-like smoke
rise from stovepipe, the thick exhaust
almost frozen in sky, I'd grasped
what I hadn't; to survive winter,
one must hug fast, grieve losses,
forgive debts, trust love, pray,
and that all who moved through
this stark bruised-hearted village
were brethren. And knowing this,
I was released. Once home, I spun
the thermostat dial past seventy,
settled in a favorite chair,
and let the warm white light
of insight melt me. Entranced
by timelessness, I began to enter
an easier, more humane season.

Nome Hoofer

HELLO CENTRAL! I rewind the tape,
replay that uncaged voice, freeze it,
and picture the flamboyant
pony-tailed New York City refugee
who arrived in Nome via Barrow.
Strange karma or what, I wonder,
to have quit the Midwest for Manhattan,
make Broadway stage, then shift
a half-dozen gears, turn to selling
barged dry goods and hardware
to salty Eskimos and whites
thousands of miles from the nearest
large downtown arts community,
somewhere you could eye a partner
like yourself on the street.

Hello yourself, I say, reaching you
through a mike. I'm leaving town,
you know. Before I do, let me guess
why you accept marking up batteries
and ropes, ringing change, directing
Music Man for a two-night stand
in a drafty gym at the world's edge.
I watched you make that corny show
work, stepping this way and that,
around and through, your dance a fancy
heel-and-toe softshoe tap. You live
for your patter; in Nome it's louder.
Am I right? Meanwhile, I'll continue
to plow straight ahead my slow talky way.
Good-bye, hoofer. The town's all yours.

Class Party, Nome

Fourteen people, eight sites,
the semester's final meeting.
From the Nome classroom, I called
attendance, kicked off festivities
by picking an Irish jig, a reel,
a New England hornpipe on mandolin.
Two young women, exchange students
from Magadan, warbled folksongs
in Russian. Next, the three guys
from prison acted a courtroom drama
they'd scripted: *Appeal to God.*
From Wales, Vince blew his harmonica,
strummed guitar, sang Woody Guthrie.
From Unalakleet Baptist Church,
Loretta played Bach. From Koyuk,
Polly told the story her grandfather
had told on his deathbed. And so on,
until Tammi from Nome counted five, four,
three, two, one, and asked everybody
everywhere to reach for the cookies
she'd mailed late last week, and munch.
It was probably Huey, from jail,
who hammed the comic smacking noises.
I closed by fiddling the E flat waltz
I'd written for those who had dropped,
who had earlier dismissed themselves.

Exit Papers, Nome

I scrawled a few lines:
fine workplace and boss,
good dean, bad chancellor,
slick university president
who I heard deliver
a commencement address
so culturally offensive
I could have heckled—
Asshole, you're in Nome;
not Long Island, New York.

And ended by scribbling
this final reflection:
Rural Alaska writing
is spirit business—
recruit teachers
who work with heart,
grace, and humility.
The surviving people
of this estranged,
endangered place
deserve no less.

And stamped the bottom
with an inky thumbprint,
sketched a rough cartoon
of a goggled musher,
dogteam pulling sled
toward a rising sun.
Caption: *Twenty-strong*
flying out of Nome,
nearing the long-sought
beauty of home.

Inner Nome

This spirit road of ghost
shrub tundra, an air current
spiraling uphill beyond fog,
wind, the memory of trees,
toward a small clearing
of blackened rock, burnt grass,
all that remains of the cabin
fire that took a life—

and continues past that spot,
past unmarked grave, gravel,
past ice, hail, drizzle, the gray
cloud countries of ancient grit,
past salmon creeks, blueberries,
reindeer, past a world shiny
and rich, the sun in love,
past everything but source.

V

Poetry Reading, Brevig Mission

Likely lured by a twenty-dollar cash prize
to be drawn afterward, half the village
gathered in the school gym's bleachers, kids
running the floor like stray marbles or molecules,
and so I began with my jokey Nome villanelle
that made some adults smile, then sawed
two fiddle tunes, then read more poems,
bowed more music as the smallest ones crawled
through my legs and their slightly older sisters
played jacks, sometimes bouncing the ball
off my ankle, until I called the children
to all join hands and circle right,
then hop back left, then lay down and snore,
then rise up dreaming they were birds,
then bears, then whales, then babies, then elders,
then teachers (here a few began punching
and kicking one another), all the while keeping
my best steady old-time beat on fiddle.
When that ten-minute round dance ended,
the parents clapped hard for the first time
all night, and I figured if I could win
half of Brevig Mission, population 230,
I could do anything, which two days later
would mean entertaining myself and one other
for part of an afternoon inside a downed plane.
But I didn't know that then when I set fiddle
in case, drew a female name that made everybody
laugh, and propelled a man and woman forward
to the lectern to thank the principal
for the dollars that would start their sweet,
little, adorable, three-month-old girl's
savings for college and career.

Plane Wreck
—in memory of Dave Rector

Mine was this easy. Flying
from Brevig Mission to Nome
into whiteness so full and dense
it was as if foglight and snow
had met and married, as if the air
was wild for cotton, the pilot flew
into a hill neither of us saw
until we sat shocked, whiplashed,
this our spectacular devastation.

Next: my blood, his panic,
the slow cold blinking of minutes
to rescue, a twenty-mile ride to town
on snowmachine. Not so bad,
really, the two days hospitalized,
my forehead swollen with three layers
of stitches, my neck in a collar,
perhaps a vertebra thinly fractured,
perhaps an unnameable,

like what had happened to a musician
I knew, a guitar-playing friend
who the same day I crashed
took a gun, aimed at himself,
fired. Oh god, he might have moaned,
as if he'd at last faced
his own particular bluish whiteness.
My plane wreck was this easy.
His illness and fear were not.

Emergency Room

—for Gary Garner

Glasses part-crooked, -bent,
-splayed, I squinted hard
into the bathroom mirror,
my face a filthy red crust
of blood and bandage. Like war,
I decided, then hobbled back
to a treatment room where a nurse
swabbed and rebandaged me,
took vitals, then wheeled me
for head and neck x-rays.
Next room, the doctor sewed me
for four hours, my six wounds
needing five kinds of stitches—
these facts, like my forehead,
a messy necessity. *A new needle—
like going through soft butter,*
I heard the doctor announce
near the end. Having learned
his patient was a curious poet
who might be inspired to write
about even this, he'd wanted
to give me a simile. I smiled
my thank-you. A good doctor,
he expected no further answer.

Concussed

There was no oh god, oh shit,
of fuck, not even a laconic
goddamnit before my plane plowed
into the hill. Just a crash
that I didn't even realize
until I came to, the pilot
dazed beside me, everything
stilled. Of course I was alive:
dead people don't put a hand
to brow, feel the blood, ask
if they are dying; dead people
don't sit inside a downed aircraft
and think—bad weather, pilot error;
dead people don't doubt their lives.

Ten days later, now complaining
of fogginess when I stood,
I lay on a message table,
felt the therapist's hands
on my temple, and saw myself
outside myself, my spirit
over the pilot's left shoulder,
my body in the co-pilot's seat,
belted in. Next instant, impact,
and my body jolted, forehead slamming
the instrument board. And I slumped
unconscious until what soul thing
that makes us human reentered
and found me brain-bruised survivor.

Brain Bruised

Like gray space, or lake confused
by squall. Or a late April fog
and mist that flurries snow.
Half-backwards logic. Frightening quiet.
A painless ache as if a slow leak,
your own warped hull. Everything out
of synch by the slightest width.
Don't turn. Close your eyes. Dream
of bandages, war-wounded children,
bullet holes in foreheads, bone
brittle as twig, broken shells, blood
and dung, lungs clotted with bugs.
Wake mornings lost in a world
bright, raw, startling, quick, cruel.
Ah, to be a cat, you think.
To experience, and shed, this life too.

In the Anchor Tavern

That next week, when I stopped in the Anchor,
always the same Bering Air pilot was quick to point:
"You know what? You're a walking dead man."
Over and over I heard him, which I admit
I liked because people noticed, I was raw,
and craved the attention those few hours
out. "It's the walking dead man, folks,"
he'd croak, hoarse from tobacco and beer.
I'd answer straight, say how I wished
I'd flown with him. "Damn right,
walking dead man," he'd say, eyes glazed,
and I hoped he was like Chilly Willie,
the Cape Smythe guy I'd flown with,
who took pains in the air, could act
moose-stupid elsewhere. "See you," I'd say,
five, or ten, or fifteen minutes later,
my coat on. "Walking dead man," he'd growl.
"Crashed into a hill. Walking dead man.
Nome's walking dead man. There he goes."

Nome Celebrity

Two years writing, teaching,
fiddling, sharing all I could,
I was known in Nome, maybe,
as one of the crazies
who rode a bike winter-long.

Then I walked from a plane crash.
Old-timers I didn't think knew me
now greeted me by name. I saw
how others watched, and whispered.
I let drunks touch me for luck.

Post-Crash Paperwork

Yesterday, when asked
my profession, I replied
"litigant," and smiled
because I was recovering
my health, would recover
completely, and had
what everyone said
was "a good case." Dumb
luck to have survived
a plane flying into a hill
at 140 mph.
     And recalled
the second night after
the accident: fearing
spine injury, doctors sat me
in a wheelchair, braced
my neck, and flew me
to Anchorage for tests.
There, at Providence,
when a nurse asked
my religion, I answered,
"poetry." For next of kin
I answered, "my readers."
For emergency contact,
I answered, "publisher
or muse, your choice."

After the Plane Crash

My second day in the hospital,
a nurse I didn't know came into
my room, shyly asked if I'd seen
the bright white light. No, I said,
then recalled that plane ride
through zero visibility where everything
had been white, grainy gauzy white,
and I'd meditated on that white,
found it inspiring, ineffable,
deep, was writing a poem in my head
about white when we hit,
and when I woke it was to blood
warm and wet down my face,
the red rinse like a movie scene.
It wasn't until a month later,
feeling like me, that I began
focusing in on light bulbs,
headlights, small shiny brightnesses
winking like stars. So this is it,
I thought, and looked harder,
taking every little last thing in.

VI

Betty's Igloo, a Bed & Breakfast

Outside, backfiring four-wheelers
or roaring snowmachines, depending
on season. Inside, appliances
barged from Seattle, knickknacks
flown from Anchorage, local beadwork,

a guestbook that has registered
Bering Straits School District teachers
from Unalakleet, Rural College deans
from Fairbanks, a freewheeling
ethnomusicologist from Switzerland.

Upstairs, the home of hosts Betty,
Mike, and son, Arlo, a family
that's built a life that withstands
Nome's mud, dust, mud, ice cycle
by practicing love, faith,

an arctic survival that celebrates
freezers of moose, trips to Hawaii,
tax shelters, the Igloo. Come visit.
In the baskets of fruit and cheese,
origami geese that fold into swans.

The Arctic Thumb
—for Maynard Perkins

Perk's job: to teach college science and math,
also one-credits in photography,
fencing, winter survival. *Follow me,*
he'd blare, rallying students, staff, that hot bath
filling at home. At least one trip a year
someplace warm. A truck in Anchorage
for those frequent flights out. His other tags—
moose hunter, pilot, unsung volunteer.
Summers, with his wife, partner who could read
his every move, he ran the Arctic Thumb,
Nome's source for soil, fertilizer, seed.
Perk's August yard: a flower garden in drums—
plus greenhouse tomatoes, zucchinis, peas.
Working the elements, he prevailed by degrees.

Big-Little Town

Next time you ride to the airport,
one more emergency trip out—
Nome to Reno, via Anchorage,
Seattle, San Francisco—cherish
this odd life so far away.

In a painful year-long autumn
of loss, the all-day commute
allows you time to refill
your soul, a small window
from twenty-two thousand feet

to thank the heavens for blessing
you with healthy husband, son,
wisdom, spirit, a warm curiosity
and compassion for every extreme
and wonderful and crazy thing.

Nome's the biggest littlest
big-little town in the world.
Where else could you have seen
so much, learned so much, done
so much for others? Rejoice.

Moving Sale

The maintenance man bought the computer
I chose not to mail. The lawyer,
the floor lamp a pain to pack.
The new teacher, my rusted
damaged town-only mountain bike.
Two friends divided my books.

I dumped banjo, kitchenware,
hardware cheap to a guy
I thought needed a break.
Likewise table, guitar, clothes.
Almost gave away stereo
and number-two village fiddle,

but the music shouted KEEP.
Ditto, my bunny boots.
Those oversized scuffed white
rubber galoshes now hung
in the living room as a memento:
I'd walked into and out of sixty below.

Twin Dragon Lunch

At my last Nome meal
I remembered how
you'd looked so rough
the first time we met,
a cold tough squint
eyeing me from across
the table, lips tight,
you having suffered
a deep monstrous pain.
I'd thought: Listen—
there's a story here.

So I did. Was that why
you'd given the books,
the print? My teacher?
Student? Friend? I saw
you soften. You saw me
smile at last. We shared
like children. Darkness
broke with each breath.
Lit by our reflections,
two torchlights flared.
Sobered, we shone.

Flight Out

Buckling yourself into your aisle seat,
flight attendant explaining what to do
if you crash, you think: You needed
this talk when you entered Nome; not now,
leaving. You've been through it,
and died. So what. And when *that* death
came, you did what you did—and nothing
could have prepared you. Now you're empty
but for the echoes of Barney toasting you
for springing this joint. Suddenly,
you feel yourself spinning, remembering
hundreds of images, like you're about
to rise, and you settle on that January night,
biking uphill across from the airport,
fiddle on your back, making a squeaky trail
through powder, ten below, windless,
en route to dinner with a woman, and you recall
how that night you heard a great roaring
in the dark—a cargo plane twice the size,
so it seemed, of any commercial jet
had fired engines. An orange flash.
A blast that made you think: Armageddon.
You'd hopped off your bike, watched the plane
accelerate and lift, the noise bigger
than a hundred square miles of tundra,
and you'd stood transfixed, thinking miracle
peak moment in your life, thinking this
was a celebration of something large
and deep breaking inside you though you knew
it was just a plane flying out of Nome
and you were just a man living a dream.

And at last your own aircraft begins to roll.

Missionary

One in a billion, I would say
of the force that sailed me
from Philadelphia to Chapel Hill
to Seattle, then Fairbanks, Juneau,
Sitka, Nome, that last spot
of northwest Alaska tundra coast
the jump-off to Savoonga,
Shishmaref, Unalakleet, Koyuk,
Stebbins, and the rest—places
I learned as I'd once learned home.

The question: Why had I traveled
such distance toting books,
a fiddle, and other white man tools?
To prove the vast sweep of wind?
To live Conrad's supreme
fictional wilderness darkness?
To report we are all kin—
a team of survivors hunting,
dreaming, gathering the edge.

Gnome

Comic, odd, unlikely, slow—
Nome's impractical joker if you will.
A strange little man with moustache
and goatee who each dawn demands
special birthday boy treatment,
pipsqueak orphan of ninety-three.

Today's present, a mirror. Look,
gnome. Your left eye's askew, winking
at the tub where you've soaked
yourself clean—check the dark ring
caked with excuses, rust, ashes, blame.
Look, your right eye's twinkling anew

with the light—some private matter,
no doubt, between you, power, wiring,
glass. Past ghost, spirit, leprechaun,
elf, watch yourself grow one foot,
two, into a handsome man opening a chest,
pulling out heart, soul, every wish.

I Jokes

In Nome we say I jokes
quick and deadpan
at the end of a joke. I jokes,

we say, the Eskimo
English sticky on tongue.
In Nome we say I jokes

all right. Could be a cluck or croak.
Or shyly, mouth covered by hand
at the end of a joke. I jokes

is how we poke
fun at our people and plans.
In Nome we say I jokes

because even though broken,
we've survived, a clan
at the end of a joke. I jokes,

we say, our spoken
coda, our last proud stand.
In Nome we say I jokes
at the end of a joke. I jokes.

Name?

Who knows, with a little luck
the white mining town on a tip
of the Seward Peninsula
might have been known as Heaven
but for the lame mapmaker
who mistook *Name?* and answered
by shaving the tail from that
small a, thus labeling the place

to rhyme with home. Nome,
a friend says to approach you
as one does a bear trap—and pass.
Another calls you the dark wound.
Myself, long-caught in nether worlds
of the devil's doing, I escape
by writing you, inhabiting you,
trashing you, releasing you.